MW01413841

*William D. Wolff*
*Illustrated by Chris Roth*

# SCREENWRITING
## *four* GENIUSES

Screenwriting four Geniuses © 2001 by William D. Wolff. All rights reserved.
A product of Wolff Productions™
P.O. Box 2322
Los Angeles, CA 90049

four Geniuses ™ Pending 2001
http://www.fourGeniuses.com
fourGeniuses@aol.com

*Layout design, Mephisto, Viagraty:* Josh Dintzer
http://www.joshstrike.com
josh@joshstrike.com
Laid primarily in Univers.

*Cover Concept:* William D. Wolff

*Illustrations:* Chris Roth
slick333@earthlink.net

*Photography:* Susan Lanier
Suzelanier@aol.com

Female models courtesy of Models, Inc.
http://www.talentmarketing.com
Blonde: Paige Brooks
Brunette: Nikki Zeno
Young male model courtesy of Michael and Mo Milder
  Young male model: Max Milder

Italicized passage in "Exposition" from <u>Body Heat</u>, © Lawrence Kasdan.

Printed in the U.S.A.

ISBN 0-9712584-0-6 (Wolff Productions)

# SCREENWRITING
## *four* GENIUSES

# TABLE of CONTENTS

*Acknowledgements* .......................................... 5

*Prologue* ................................................... 7

*Section 1: Story* .......................................... 11
    Selecting a Theme or Genre        14
    Comedy        15
    High Concept - Your Ticket Out of the Ghetto        17
    Titles        19
    Essential Story Ingredients        21
    The 3-Act Structure and Other Hoaxes        25
    The Myth of Conflict        27
    2$^{nd}$ Act Problems        30
    The Shattering Conclusion        32

*Section 2: Character* ..................................... 35
    Character Types        38
    Character Names        40
    Creating Vivid Characterizations        41

*Section 3: Dialogue* ...................................... 43
    Writing Character-Specific Dialogue        47
    Parentheticals        49
    Writing the Star Vehicle        52

*Section 4: Exposition* .................................... 55

*Section 5: Movie Trivia Quiz!* ............................ 59

*Section 6: Proper Screenplay Format* ...................... 65
    Get Visual, Already!        68
    Spelling        69
    Punctuation        71

**Section 7: Miscellaneous Tricks of the Trade** .................... **73**
    Subtext        76
    Subplots        79
    Backstory        81
    The "Beat" - Misunderstood, Misused
        and Mispronounced        83
    Product Placement        85

**Section 8: Writing for Television** .............................. **87**

**Section 9: Ask the Expert!** .................................... **93**

**Section 10: Let's Get to Work!** ................................ **99**
    Getting Started        102
    The Pharmacology of Inspiration        103
    Get Out of That Rut        107
    Begging, Borrowing and Your 1st Amendment Rights        109

**Section 11: Playing the Hollywood Game -**
**And Kicking Serious Butt!** ................................ **111**
    Getting Past the Professional Reader        114
    Getting an Agent        116
    Development Heaven        118

**Section 12: Beyond Success** .................................. **121**
    Giving Back to the Community - In Spades        126

**About the Author** ............................................ **130**

# ACKNOWLEDGEMENTS

The author would like to thank the following for their contributions to this book. My father-in-law, Walton Harris, and my brother-in-law, Geoffrey Harris, have both given me valuable encouragement and critical comments. Thanks also to Dr. Dennis Palumbo, whose insight into the creative process and into the practical considerations involved in putting together a project like this have been invaluable.

Special thanks to my daughters, Lena and Jessee, for their love and for their appreciation of my creative efforts. I'm one lucky guy.

Especially, I express my love and appreciation for my wife, Brooke, without whose remarkable generosity, critical judgement and unflagging support it would not have been possible for me to pursue my creative ambitions.

# PROLOGUE

### The Myth:

With the sink overflowing with dirty dishes, the supportive but beleaguered wife sits at the cramped dinner table, laboring over a foot-high stack of bills. Sighing decisively, she resolves to buy time by cramming the check for the phone bill into the gas company's envelope, by intentionally neglecting to sign the electric bill, and by concocting a fiendishly muddled explanation of just why the mortgage is not technically due until after the 15$^{th}$ of next month.

The preternaturally wizened children huddle around a 10-inch, black-and-white TV, at best a marginally effectual insulation against the horrors of onrushing maturity.

A clenched stream of profanity erupts from the smoke-filled den, propelling the loyal but prematurely arthritic cocker spaniel under the kitchen table, where he lies quivering, a cottony froth of saliva congealing around his abscessed jowls.

Ensconced within this windowless den, wracked by a dry, tubercular cough as he hunches over his creaky Underwood, is The Writer, wrestling with his inner demons. Only a fifth of Early Times, a pack of Lucky Strikes and a fistful of Phenobarbital stands between The Writer and that terrifying, blank page. Armed with the wisdom borne of decades laboring at his craft, The Writer no longer demands of himself brilliance, inspiration or even luck, but only a moment's respite from the omnipresent, stentorian voice of his father, an ex-semi-pro hockey player, who was felled by a massive coronary only 2 weeks before his retirement after 40 years as an underwriter for Consolidated Title...

Such is the prevailing image of the writer's tormented life, in which he toils in obscurity and poverty against stupefying odds, occasionally managing to land an assignment rewriting classified ads for waitresses seeking work in the sex trade in their spare time.

## The Reality:

But nothing could be further from the truth. These days, it is far more likely that the writer's biggest problem is not writer's block, but writer's cramp - from having to sign such a great proliferation of ever-more colossal checks.

The secret is finally getting out that for nearly fifty years, but especially in the last decade, there has been a tremendous abundance of opportunities for Hollywood screenwriters. Protective of their golden goose, those in the know have engaged in a cynical but effective campaign of disinformation, attempting to dissuade potential rivals from entering this phenomenally lucrative field.

The shameless perpetrators of this fraud, among them Robert McKee (Story), Neil D. Hicks (Screenwriting 101), Syd Field (Screenplay), Linda Seger (Making a Good Movie Great) and David R. Trottier (The Screenwriter's Bible, for Christ's sake! Have these unrepentant misanthropes no shame?), have made countless millions by cynically stacking the deck in their own favor.

An indication of the devastation these sadists have wrought is the burgeoning crop of hack psychologists and pill-pushing psychiatrists, whose waiting rooms from Encino to Beverly Hills are packed with borderline-suicidal aspiring screenwriters, who can soon add imminent bankruptcy to their sad litany of woe.

First, these self-serving charlatans seduce their innocent victims with grandiose promises of great wealth, thunderous critical acclaim and the rapturous joy of artistic fulfillment.

Then, once the bait is taken, these same predators proceed to emasculate their prey, convincing them that writing a great screenplay is extremely difficult and that the odds of success are virtually nil. In this manner, they have created an inexhaustible demand for their services, as they criss-cross the globe in their Gulfstream Fives, leaving a gruesome trail of shattered dreams, mortgaged homes and exhausted prostitutes in their wake.

One myth perpetrated by this cabal of conspiring cowards is that there are vast hordes of aspiring screenwriters, churning out tens of thousands of scripts each year, competing for the attention of a few overburdened executives. While it may be true that hundreds, perhaps even thousands, of hopeful writers begin a screenplay each year, in actual fact over 99% of screenplays begun are never even finished, usually having gotten bogged down in the mire of the dreaded $2^{nd}$ act (a diabolical invention of these same purveyors of the status quo, one which the aspiring screenwriter need never fear after reading this modest treatise).

Another such blatant untruth is that there are only a small number of stories available, and that these have already been written and re-written into the ground. (The number usually given - seven - is, not surprisingly, a prime number, known to induce hypothermia, copious bleeding from the eye sockets and numbness of the sexual organs.) Just scan the 100 million-plus films produced in the last 20 years looking for the word "Story" in the title, and you will come up with thousands, if not billions, of entries.

But perhaps the most laughably false assertion is that writing a terrific screenplay is difficult and time-consuming. The modest goal of this treatise is to, once and for all, dispel this pernicious myth.

First, the typical screenplay is only 120 pages long - about 1/3 the size of an average novel (which, admittedly, can take up to 2 or 3 months to write). And, like the ever-decreasing age, attention span and career expectancy of your typical studio executive, the maximum permissible number of pages is shrinking every day.

Second, well over half of the usable space on the page is blank. (The authorities certainly have a knack for making their own lives easier!)

Third, the supposedly difficult task of writing dialogue has been reduced to child's play, due to the progressive shrinking of its margins. (We estimate that by the time this book is published, dialogue will already have been reduced to roughly 1.5 column inches.) Further, well over half of the space occupied by dialogue must now be peppered with profanity, exclamation points and parentheticals (explicit directions to the befuddled actor: "Passionately"; "Rolling his eyes").

In this essay, we will for the first time lift the veil of secrecy which has shrouded the art and business of screenwriting. We will demystify such forbidding concepts as "character arc" (there is - or should be - no such thing); "catalytic character" (confusing characterization with the $3^{rd}$ law of thermodynamics); and "slug line" (used interchangeably with "inciting incident"). Within hours, you will be creating memorable characters, writing sparkling dialogue and churning out "high concept" screenplays at a rate limited solely by your typing ability.

With just a little bit of luck, before long you will be cavorting with the "beautiful people," as armies of nubile, scantily clad, undocumented aliens toil in your labyrinthine hilltop estate. Never again will you wait in line at the DMV, never again will you have to endure the indignity of having your spelling corrected, or even observed. Cellulite, periodontal disease and that pustulating tumor in your rectum will be things of the past, as you enter a world of gleaming white teeth, unimaginably obscene affluence and perpetual sexual gratification.

So, let's just jump right in!

# SECTION 1: STORY

# I

As stupid, misinformed and downright sadistic as all the other self-proclaimed experts in the art of screenwriting in fact are, we would be remiss not to acknowledge that there is one thing on which we agree: If you're going to write a movie, you're going to need a story. But alas, our pleasant instant of agreement with these fellows must be brief, as if this single, infinitesimal brush with objective reality has apparently been sufficiently unnerving to cause these fools to retreat into ever more irrelevant spheres of obfuscation and self-referential gibberish.

## Selecting a Theme or Genre

Before you actually start typing, it is advisable to have at least a general theme in mind, such as "Sex," "Lesbian Sex" or "Hot Lesbian Sex." But if this proves too difficult - or too limiting - there's nothing wrong with starting with only a genre. And even here, don't worry too much about getting specific right now. Many Hollywood movies have gone on to become extremely successful without fitting into any particular genre.

For example: Silence of the Lambs - is it an Elizabethan costume drama, or the pilot for a spinoff of "The Naked Chef?" Chinatown - a documentary about the exploitation of our natural resources, or a frothy sexual romp? You get the idea.

The most important thing is to start typing as soon as possible, without the process being derailed by preconceptions, misconceptions, or, for that matter, by any type of conceptions at all.

## Comedy

But let's say that even coming up with a genre proves daunting. Not to worry! When in doubt, you can't go wrong selecting comedy.

From the beleaguered studio executive, in constant terror of losing his job and spending the rest of his days rattling around in his 40,000 square-foot Bel-Air estate, watching his golden parachute being sucked into the offshore accounts of his revolving squad of $10,000-a-night prostitutes, to the lowly reader, herself better educated than her boss yet paradoxically unfulfilled in the deeper sense of things, these people are all longing for a laugh, a simple reprieve from the stresses of their day-to-day lives.

All the aspiring comedy writer needs is the ability to tell a joke, or, lacking that, the ability to laugh at one. And, as the recent spate of gross-out teen comedies demonstrates, for a comedy to be immensely successful it doesn't necessarily have to be funny. Making the writer's task even easier, the strategically placed occurrence of flatulence or projectile vomiting rarely fails to inject a cathartic levity into the most depressingly pedestrian proceedings.

But never make the grievous error of confusing satire for comedy. Such potential comic greats as Terry Southern and Paddy Chayefsky have seen their careers and reputations ruined by indulging in this pretentious, nasty genre.

Take Dr. Strangelove. In the hands of a true comic visionary such as Jerry Bruckheimer, this dismal exercise could have been a fast-paced, special-effects extravaganza, with legions of Baywatch-type babes scampering through the mall, screaming as their clothing is seared off one delicious layer after another, all played out against a backdrop of eye-popping thermonuclear blasts and eardrum-rupturing techno-funk music.

Instead, Dr. Strangelove is a solemn affair, inhabited by colorless, paunchy males sitting around the War Room watching all the "action" unfold on a large screen.

As further indication of the problems which beset this troubled production, apparent budgetary constraints forced at least one beleaguered and bewildered actor to play multiple roles; we squirm in embarrassment when we see such unrealistic demands being placed upon an actor of such limited range as Sterling Hayden. (One would think the filmmakers would have had a clue of the tremendous odds they were up against, had they noted at the start that the screenplay had been written entirely in black-and-white.)

Dr. Strangelove's misguided director, Stanley Kramer, said that he intended the audience to find itself in a moral quagmire at the end of the movie, simultaneously rooting for the American pilots to drop the bomb and appalled by the consequent annihilation of all life as we know it. That the film accomplishes this goal in spades inadvertently reveals satire's fatal flaw: Rather than being inspired to screw each others' brains out after the show, the viewing couple finds their raging hormones rendered quiescent, sapped of all their adolescent effervescence, as they engage in snippy, pseudo-philosophical bickering, just like their repressed, downtrodden parents.

## High Concept - Your Ticket out of the Ghetto

No, we aren't going to belabor the hackneyed joke that a high concept screenplay is the result of the writer being high on illicit drugs.

But, sometimes we wish he had been.

Let's examine <u>Jaws</u>, a film that really had no right to be as immensely successful as it almost was. Breaking down this one-note clunker to its essential ingredient (note that we pointedly do not use the plural, "ingredients"), we come up with: A Big Shark Eats People. So, what else is new? Alas, as the movie-going public is an easily manipulated and fundamentally bewildered herd, they flocked to this predictable mess by the hundreds.

Just as an exercise, let's explore how the decidedly low concept idea behind <u>Jaws</u> could have been modified to turn it into a real mega-hit, one that could have changed the future course of mainstream cinema. The idea is to take a familiar thematic element and to juxtapose it with a contrasting element, thus creating a wildly original new cinematic creation.

First, we observe that the idea of a giant shark is not too bad in and of itself. Primordial creatures like dinosaurs and Negroes always seem to capture the imagination of the movie-going public; and "raising the stakes" by making things bigger than they actually are in "real life" is a time-honored tradition in Hollywood. The conceit of this shark eating youngsters wearing skimpy bathing suits also seems to work, injecting a human element, as well as erotic tension, into the story, in addition to opening up opportunities for all kinds of innovative, stomach-churning gore.

So, what's missing? Well, I (actually, my personal assistant), for one, am getting mighty tired of all the action taking place in this vast, placid body of water, undulating lazily and without any sense of the high stakes inner turmoil I (my personal assistant) require to keep from nodding off or dusting off my (my personal assistant's) Tec-9. Perhaps the words "high stakes" are giving me a clue...Yes! We'll put the shark in...Las Vegas! It's <u>Jaws</u> meets <u>Bugsy</u> (and here's our title: <u>Jawsy</u>)!

Now our imagination really takes off, as we zero in upon exactly where in Las Vegas our action will take place. Should it be the MGM Grand? No, too family oriented, not enough intimation of the rotting underbelly of roiling human passions. It must be Caesar's Palace! Noting its conspicuous decadence and its abundance of prostitutes and gangsters (probably wearing sharkskin suits!), we realize we've struck upon a high concept idea that will practically write itself.

Now that our creative juices are really flowing, let's take a crack at another film which failed to live up to its potential: <u>Alien</u>. We note that the probable reason for this film's dismal showing was its predictability: An Alien Monster in Outer Space - what did you expect to find up there, the Amish? (We do, however, acknowledge the clever touch of making our alien a female.)

What if we take the monster from <u>Alien</u> and put her on...well, why not an Amish farm!? <u>Alien</u> meets <u>Witness</u> - it's <u>Alienitis</u>! (See what a snap this brainstorming is?) We can practically smell those buxom, milk-fed Amish lasses, glistening with sweat as they scurry about the cornfields, while their menfolk, with their muttonchops and pointy hats, run around yodeling and ringing bells and such. But then, we think about our poor monster, stuck in this cultural wasteland, with no television and no cellular phone. What if she has a sudden urge for some alien take-out? And, how is she going to get home to her family? We visualize her weeping great, boogery tears, and suddenly it becomes clear: The Alien is our protagonist! And by the time her spaceship is fixed, her Amish co-stars will have taught her some valuable lesson to take back home with her, something having to do with proper table manners, or everybody pitching in together at the goddamn crack of dawn.

## Titles

Coming up with a terrific title is essential to grabbing the potential paying viewer's attention. The title should suggest a sense of both novelty and familiarity, piquing the viewer's curiosity while simultaneously reassuring him that he will not be challenged in any untoward manner. A title that captures these two virtues virtually cries out, "See me," or, failing that, "See me again."

Scientific studies have conclusively demonstrated that certain "hot words" never fail to attract the attention of even the most phlegmatic reader. Among those time-tested keywords are: "Sex," "Young," "Hot," "Death," "Deadly," "Fatal," "Lethal," "Mutant," "Alien," "Hell," "Anaerobic" and "Teen."

Juxtaposing one of these can't-miss keywords with a pleasingly grating, contrasting word or phrase elicits an immediate sense of engaged confusion, which will have them reaching for their wallets:

1. Lethal Contraption
2. Deadly Inflection
3. Hot Teenage Alien Virus Sex Sluts From Hell
4. Lethal Young Mutant Sex Sluts of Virus Death
5. Fatal Abscess

The astute reader, perceiving the similarity between titles 3 and 4 above, might ask, "What's the difference between these 2 films?" And, indeed, there is very little difference. The idea is, why constantly re-invent the wheel? Once you've got a good thing going, stick with it.

Now, extend this simple truism one step further, and apply the same reasoning to the writing of the actual screenplay itself. Taking the most successful elements from Hot Teenage... and using the "Cut and Paste" technology found on many modern computers, the writer can simply rearrange these proven ingredients. Then, using "Search and Replace," he can change the names around. And, voila! In this manner, he will have created a vibrant, original new screenplay in its own right: <u>Lethal Young</u>...

Thus, a phenomenally lucrative new "franchise" is born.

## Essential Story Ingredients

Absent certain essential ingredients, even the most skillfully written, original, profound and entertaining screenplay will never earn its author a dime. The astute reader must bear with us, as we deign to enumerate these critical story elements for the benefit of our culturally challenged or intellectually impaired readers.

A story needs:

1. Sex, especially lesbian sex
2. Fast cars
3. Explosions
4. Money
5. Extreme violence and death
6. Comic relief

Let's take these points one by one.

1. Sex. We assume of our reader a minimal complement of functioning synapses, and we expect no debate over the absolute necessity of sex. The only question is how much. And the answer is, as much as possible, period. So, the cynical pragmatist might ask, why not just write a porno movie, with wall-to-wall sex and no plot whatsoever? Because, you uncultured degenerate, we are artists. And, as such, we have a responsibility to portray precisely

in what context our wall-to-wall sex will occur.

So, why lesbian sex? Well, no red-blooded American male wants to be compared to some beefy stud, better-looking and better-endowed than he is. And it is a universally acknowledged truth that this same male's single most cherished fantasy is to have sex with 2 or more women simultaneously. Moreover, notwithstanding the hysterical shrieking of a flock of ball-busting bull dykes, this same male will surely pick up the tab for tonight's flick; he has every right to demand that his date look and behave exactly like the sluts on screen, when she and her baby sister return the favor in the back seat after the show.

2. Fast cars. Anyone can write a scene containing a Ferrari (but watch out for that tricky spelling!). The secret here is to demonstrate your intimacy with your story elements and your superiority over your reader by properly identifying its compression ratio in cubic centimeters, its ignition firing sequence in foot-pounds per lunar cycle, etc.

3. Explosions. There have been so many explosions throughout the history of film that the writer might despair of ever injecting any originality into this vital story element. But a moment's contemplation reveals an abundance of untapped variations. For example, who has yet seen a super-slo-mo, extreme close-up of a baby hummingbird's eyeball exploding from the inside out, with its delicate tendrils of blood-flecked vitreous humor arcing gracefully through space? Or, try to remember the last time you saw a box of Rice Krispies the size of the Empire State Building being bombarded by a hailstorm of petrified extraterrestrial plasma.

Finally, if you're in a pinch, perhaps facing a seemingly impossible deadline; or, if you're striving for the refreshingly unexpected impact resulting from calculated stupidity, you may simply alter a generic explosion thus:

Instead of this:

KABOOM!

Write this:

KAAAAAAAAAAAAAAAABOOOOOOOOOOOOOOOOOOOOO
OOOOOOOOOOOOOOOOOOOOOOOOOOOOOOOOOOOOOOO
OOOOOOOOOOOOMMMMMMMMMMMM!!!!!!!!!!!!!!

Rest assured, your reader will feel the tremendous pain delivered by this expertly crafted blast.

4. Money. Since even those screenplays written by utter novices will contain many references to money, what separates the seasoned professional from the dilettante is the quantity thereof. Therefore, before sending your screenplay out to be read, examine every reference to money and slide the decimal point 7 or 8 places to the right. (But be consistent. Remember, your reader's lack of intelligence is inversely proportional to her abundant anal retentiveness, and you must never overlook the likelihood that she always keeps a calculator handy, and that she will keep count. Don't let some silly mathematical inconsistency slip through the cracks and ruin your career before it has even begun!)

Assuming your math checks out, you have now "upped the stakes," so that even the most jaded reader cannot help but feel an urgent need to get to the end, to find out how things eventually turn out.

5. Extreme violence and death. See explosions.

6. Comic relief. Even the grimmest of dramas must contain some instance of levity, to remind the viewer that great hilarity can be found in even the most profound misery suffered by others. In <u>Sophie's Choice</u>, the climactic scene, in which the Nazi General forces

the Della Street character to choose between her son and her daughter, rarely fails to generate at least a hearty snicker from the audience. Because, possibly lured into the theater by the title's subtle suggestion of lesbian sex (see above), yet increasingly dismayed by the prospect that this may have been a cynical ruse on the filmmaker's part, the target audience of 11- to 17-year-old males is now tremendously relieved by the intimation that the aforementioned sex might just involve a mother-and-daughter team.

## The 3-Act Structure and Other Hoaxes

Under the cynical subterfuge of such lofty titles as "Expert Story Consultant," unrepentant sadists such as Robert McKee have made countless millions shamelessly promoting a slavish adherence to the "traditional" 3-act structure. Citing examples from Neanderthal cave paintings, through Shakespeare and up to such muddled contemporary works as Casablanca (to this day, no one knows whether this film has a happy ending or not; in fact, no one is certain this meandering mess even has an ending at all, instead culminating in little more than a hill of beans), these standard bearers of the status quo have done more to inhibit the creativity of the aspiring screenwriter than a stack of rejections from a pack of persnickety (and probably homosexual) junior executives.

As odious as this task will be, we trust that the reader will discern the higher purpose in our delineating the fundamental tenets of this loathsome construct.

Act I - Conflict
Act II - Complications
Act III - Resolution

Or, in the colloquial parlance:

Act I - Boy meets Girl
Act II - Boy loses Girl
Act III - Boy gets Girl back

Now, compare these 2 variations. Inconsistencies abound right out of the gate: "Boy meets Girl" - this is a conflict? "Boy loses Girl" - how complicated is this? "Boy gets Girl Back" - What if the Boy has fallen in love with someone else, or has been rendered a eunuch by some intergalactic cosmic ray? What if several years have passed (as when the film is some kind of sweeping epic)? The Girl will now be in her mid-20s, her looks will be gone, and her usefulness as an object of romantic obsession or sexual degradation will be nil.

Furthermore, a number of newer films have forever laid to rest the necessity of adhering to so archaic and constricting a game plan. In <u>Pulp Fiction</u>, characters die and are resurrected later on, with no visible scars or any indication of the psychological trauma which would likely accompany such a disconcerting ordeal. In <u>Memento</u>, the entire movie begins at the end and ends at the beginning, although it's a mystery how this can occur when each individual scene progress from beginning to end (perhaps this is to allay suspicions that the film was accidentally shipped to theaters before having been rewound).

Had the writers of <u>Pulp Fiction</u> and <u>Memento</u> slavishly adhered to the stultifying, traditional 3-act structure, these films would certainly never have attained their great critical acclaim and commercial success; indeed, their main claim to fame might have been their archtypically pedestrian plot lines.

## The Myth of Conflict

Reactionaries like Mr. McKee et al are always crowing, "Drama is conflict." Or, "Conflict is drama." Now, if these alleged authorities can't even figure out which one is which, then it's a fairly safe bet they haven't the foggiest idea what they're talking about.

According to these pundits, some "inciting incident" launches our protagonist into an escalating struggle against titanic forces, against which he must summon up inner resources he never knew he had, in order to occupy our attention during the next 60 minutes or so of our lives. And in the end, they assert, having been contorted through some so-called "character arc," ("arch" is the word you're groping for, Gentlemen; or, perhaps it's "ark"), he either may or may not succeed, depending, presumably, on whether the movie is a comedy or a tragedy.

A good example of a reasonably successful film which had none of this formulaic "conflict" these experts claim to be so essential is Andy Warhol's Sleep. (An indication of this film's success is that it is quite well-known, even to those who have never actually seen it; and many of these non-viewers are familiar with not only its basic plot line, but also with such obscure details as its running time.)

The only element of conflict in the conventional sense is the inciting incident: Our protagonist gets tired. After that, Sleep contains no particular antagonist of any import, except for that pesky, protruding spring in the upper left; when presented with an obstacle to overcome, such as a limb going numb, our protagonist merely shifts his position slightly; and by the end he has undergone no cataclysmic inner transformation, except for having an urgent desire to urinate.

Just for fun, let's apply a little of what we have learned so far, just to see how a more commercially attuned Mr. Warhol might have transformed Sleep from a moderate box-office hit into a commercial sensation:

If Mr. Warhol had had even a modicum of commercial instincts, he would have edited the screenplay for <u>Sleep</u> down to 10 minutes and retitled it <u>Catnap</u>. Then, he would have fired his 25-year-old male actor and recast the film with a pair of prepubescent, 14-year-old ingenues clad in skimpy, Victoria's Secret satin negligees. But now our title is sounding more than a little provincial, so we change it to: <u>Hot Young Sex Kittens of Mutant Coma Slut</u>.

We now fire our union production designer, drive over to Le Sex Shoppe on Santa Monica Blvd. and pick up a few props (and some pointers on how to use them). We dump our 55-year-old, half-blind cameraman, who has been malingering around this town for as long as possible, in order to collect on his undeserved pension. We get our old Arriflex out of the attic and smear the lens with Vaseline, for that gauzy, late-night cable TV, soft-porn effect (the aggressive marketing campaign is already congealing in our mind's eye).

And now, we calculate (numbers are a big deal in this business!): At a 10-minute running time, at 4 showings per hour there could have been 4 X 10 hours = 40 showings per day. Assuming <u>Hot Young</u>... had shown on 2000 screens nationwide; and further assuming the theatres had been filled at 150 seats per showing (¾ of an average 200-seat multiplex theater), we get:

(40 showings) X (2000 screens) X (150 seats per screen) = 12,000,000 tickets sold per day.

12,000,000 X ($9.00 per ticket) = $108,000,000 per day.

$108,000,000 X (7 days) = $756 million (domestic) in <u>Hot Young</u>...'s first week alone.

Now, to perform the intricate regression analysis we pump the numbers through 12 parallel Cray Series 9 supercomputers, and we calculate that, given a 12-week span in theatres, and then factoring in ancillary rights (whatever they are), video rentals, cable TV sales, foreign ticket sales, syndication rights, Internet streaming, action figures and edible panties, our new, leaner and meaner Hot Young... is likely to generate roughly $12.725 billion, thus supplanting such classics as Twister, and even Pokemon, as the new cinematic standard by which all others will be judged.

(Alas, Mr. Warhol is chiefly remembered for having created an obscure series of paintings of Campbell's soup cans, which received desultory critical and commercial acclaim in their day. Had he been sufficiently prescient to foresee the unflagging interest in all things Cosa Nostra, Mr. Warhol would have chosen Progresso soup as his model, and would have made an indelible impression on the art world, not to mention having been able to afford a decent haircut.)

## 2nd Act Problems

As we mentioned earlier, many a potential Shane Black or Zane Grey has come up with a vibrant, high-concept idea, launched into his 1st Act with a vengeance and come up with an opening of explosive tension, only to be stopped dead in his tracks upon having entered the dreaded 2nd Act.

(We know, we know. Earlier on, we disavowed the necessity of dealing with 1st or 2nd Acts, or with Acts of any variety whatsoever. We're just testing our publisher, confident in our assessment of this peculiar animal, certain as the day is long that by now he is not reading past the chapter headings. Just for fun, watch this: "Hey, Mr. Doubleday/Knopf! Your mother wears army boots!" We rest our case.)

As we were saying, this alleged 2nd Act has proven the undoing of many an aspiring great. How much simpler life would be if we could state the problem and then just go ahead and solve it, without having to go through all these often tedious "dramatic" gyrations!

But wait! There is nothing inherently wrong with this sentiment. And it in fact suggests one ingenious way around this whole conundrum: Simply elongate the ending of the beginning problem section, attach it to a similarly stretched-out beginning of the ending resolution section and forget about the middle section entirely. Then, just submit the damn thing to your agent, and wait for your check to arrive. If some wise-ass D-Girl should have the nerve to ask how your 1st Act ends, without a moment's hesitation proclaim, "Page fucking 40. Or page fucking 35. How the fuck should I know? And, what were your alternate career plans?" As she stammers in flabbergasted bewilderment, blow a perfect smoke ring and wheel away with an appropriately contemptuous sneer.

Now, we acknowledge that the above strategy may not cut the mustard with our more finicky readers, or with those for whom the concept of the free-wheeling writer, responsible only to the beckoning call of his muse, grates harshly against their infantile, Protestant sensibilities. For these perpetually morose malcontents, we offer a few alternatives.

The use of certain "off-the-shelf" complications, which through repeated use have become accepted cinematic conventions, can generally get you out of a tight spot. Here is an abridged list of these items, which when plopped into your screenplay rarely fail to achieve the desired effect:

Brain tumor/pregnancy
Evil twin
Crazed Vietnam vet
Ocean liner, aircraft carrier or any other extremely large object
Michael Madsen

We encourage the reader to not merely uncritically insert one or more of these tried and true wrinkles into his work, but to experiment with variations which will add texture and, if executed properly, may actually result in glaucoma or irritable bowel syndrome.

## The Shattering Conclusion

OK! We've ratcheted up the stakes to such a degree that our audience is squirming in their seats, some members actually vomiting blood or experiencing coronary thrombosis.

Our hero, Rik, is standing on the desolate moon of some God-forsaken planet hundreds of billions of light-years from Earth, surrounded by 800 aliens with 72 rows each of razor-sharp teeth, armed with cosmic rays, all shrieking in their high-pitched alien whine:

>               ALIENS
>       (shrieking; rolling their eyes)
>   ※⌇⁻⊣⟨⅔⟩ˇ⋀⋀◉⥋⋔!!   ◎⥋⊞⊞⋔⌇⁻¾/⇟⇝ˇˇˇ!!?*!ˇ
>       (subtitled)
>   "Riiiiiiiik!  You got some 'splainin'
>   to do!!!**?*!"

How are we going to wrap this thing up? How will Rik get out of this mess? Surely, it's hopeless!

But suddenly, a donut-shaped, 750 square-mile Lincoln safe, wandering aimlessly through space from Alpha Centauri for the last 400,000 eons, materializes out of the ionosphere and crashes to the ground, crushing every one of the aliens and leaving Rik standing untouched in the center, panting triumphantly amid a swirling cloud of radioactive dust and fizzy, vaporized alien innards. Rik has done it! He has triumphed!

"Now, hold on a minute!" we can already hear the chorus of lily-livered, limp-wristed traditionalists wail. "You can't do that! That's just *deus ex machina*!" Then they will go on to sputter about how some mere coincidence, a supposed contrivance concocted by the irresponsible writer, has miraculously intervened, relieving Rik of having to summon up the inner resources required to prevail against these overwhelming odds (resources he never knew he had, in case

Story | 33

you were wondering). Next thing you know, these same crybabies will be blubbering about *character arc*, and those asinine *psychological underpinnings* of theirs and God knows what else, and finally we righteously exclaim, "Shut the fuck up!"

Let's examine this *deus ex machina* idea a little more closely: "*Deus ex machina*," literally translated, means "two not machines" (or "several 1953 Chryslers"). "Two not machines"??? Now, if this is the most coherent explanation these imbeciles can come up with for why we brilliant, inspired artists should not be permitted free access to our fertile imaginations, then how they expect to be taken seriously is the real mystery here.

Listen here, we want to tell these creatively emasculated eunuchs, we love the movies precisely because they transport us into a world where anything can and will happen, as opposed to the oppressive, tedious predictability of ordinary life. Here, day after ever-lovin' day we are beaten into the ground by the shrill carping of our dumpy wife and the incessant whining of our snotty kids and the synapse-rattling braying of our slobbery, good-for-nothing basset hound, so we grease up the thirty-odd-six, we blow them all over the walls, we get caught and we fry in the electric chair. In the movies, we get away with it, cash in on that $100 million insurance policy and live in unimaginable splendor for the rest of our lives. This is what we want!  For Christ's sake, let us have it!

# SECTION 2: CHARACTER

# II

The common wisdom holds that every screenplay must contain a protagonist, an antagonist, and a romantic interest. The fallacy in this argument is laid bare by the observation that all that's needed to induce vast legions of adolescent males to flock to the theater is one naked female and a few electromagnetic or thermonuclear devices. (With a flourish of political correctness, we observe that to lure young females into the theaters all you need is one half-naked, hermaphroditic male with a mop of blonde hair and a pronounced absence of muscle tone - Leonardo DiCaprio, for example.)

But it is a testament to the inordinate political power of the Teamster's Union and their mercenary lackeys in the Screen Actors Guild that 9 out of 10 of the films showing at your local multiplex contain 1 or more ostensibly human characters. If you want to be a "player," you had better resign yourself to working within this communist-inspired limitation.

## Character Types

As is often the case, however, what initially appears to be an annoying, arbitrary constraint can be made to work to your advantage. The central characters in all movies are all "types," that come with built-in attributes and motivations, and are laden with certain role-specific "psychological underpinnings," a meaningless term invented by critics to propagate their own confusion and to intimidate their reader(s).

All the writer has to do is take each of these generic characters, give him a couple of distinctive, identifiable characteristics (such as a lisp, or a list - preferably to the left) and plunk him right into his screenplay.

Anyone who goes to the movies with any regularity will intuitively recognize the traits that go with each of these archetypal characters. Let's take a little test, one which is impossible to fail, which will conclusively demonstrate this fact. Just match the characters on the left with the corresponding adjectives on the right:

|                          |                        |
|--------------------------|------------------------|
|                          | a. shiftless           |
|                          | b. tendentious         |
|                          | c. New and Improved!   |
| 1. protagonist           | d. unctuous            |
|                          | e. lugubrious          |
|                          | f. Sharon Stone        |
|                          | g. apoplectic          |
|                          | h. flaccid             |
| 2. antagonist            | i. differently         |
|                          | j. easily digested     |
|                          | k. fulsome             |
|                          | l. topography          |
|                          | m. white               |
| 3. romantic interest     | n. putrid              |
|                          | o. slovenly            |
|                          | p. young               |
|                          | q. hot                 |
|                          | r. astigmatic          |
|                          | s. ectoplasm           |
|                          | t. saturnine           |
| (Answers appear on page 372.) |                    |

And that's all there is to it. Now, all you have to do is add the various tics, physical deformities and psychopathic idiosyncrasies required to give the reader a sense of identification with your characters.

# Character Names

Coming up with names which suggest the gender, emotional underpinnings and size of your characters goes a long way toward relieving you of having to justify, or even understand, their behavior in any tortured, logical way. Avoid such generic, colorless names as "David," "Michael" and "Uma;" or, if there is some compelling reason for using them (such as a faulty key on your keyboard), at least make the effort to spell them in creative, evocative ways: "Dahvood," "Mihell," "Uma."

Here are some suggestions which will get you on the right track:

White male protagonist: "Rik," "Nik," "Rok" - all these names suggest a beefy, Midwestern muscularity, an ingratiating stupidity poised for immediate, senseless violence.

White female romantic interest: "Riki," "Niki," "Roki" - the submissive lubricity required of these roles is well-conveyed.

African-American male: "Ri'ik," "Ni'ik," "Ro'ok" - for variation, substitute a comma or an exclamation point for the apostrophe.

Antagonist: "Pric," "Spic," "Dik" - these names impart the appropriate sense of swarthy menace and oily dread.

African-American female: "Ru'uby," "Sa'apphire," "O'oprah" - earthy and lustful, yet subliminally mendacious.

Miscellaneous ethnic types: "Hung Dong," "Big Nipper" - playfully reversing the common stereotype of the undernourished, poorly endowed Oriental.

Miscellaneous extraterrestrial types: "Gork," "Dork," "Rourke."

## Creating Vivid Characterizations

In his unintentionally hilarious book, Pure Drivel, novice writer and ersatz comedian, Steve Martin, offers the following advice regarding the art of creating memorable characters: "Nothing will make your writing soar more than a memorable character." So what's wrong with his analysis? Actually, nothing. We only bring it up to point out that Mr. Martin severely undermines his case by failing to catch a typographical error right in the title itself. Stevie, Baby! If you're going to write about basketball, learn the moves!

(Lest the reader suspect sour grapes, let me assure him that Steverino and I are old chums, having spent many a pleasant evening on Ibiza playing a gentlemanly game of backgammon. But, truth be told, he can be counted upon to fall for the rudimentary Varney Counter-Gambit whenever he's had 5 or 6 Martinis - ironically, his biggest weakness.)

Such misanthropes as McKee (see above, if you must) advise the writer to introduce one's characters with a brief description, some identifying characteristics for the reader to hang his hat on, to coin a phrase. Amid all the drivel (Mr. Martin, take note of the proper use of this word!) dispensed by such charlatans, an occasional morsel of truth can be found. But this isn't one of them.

Mr. Martin takes a step in the right direction, reducing this convoluted principle to what might at first appear to be its bare necessity: Give your character a "trait." Still, this misguided altruism, adroitly disguised as fuzzy thinking, only succeeds in overcomplicating the issue.

Just give him an ethnic stereotype, or a weight (weight is technically not a "trait," but, rather, a unique identifying characteristic of that character's unique identity; we are what we eat), and let it go at that.

When the reader reads:

    JAMA'AL  (Jewish)

...he immediately know that Jama'al is a shifty, dangerous fellow, that he has tremendous leaping ability and that he is surely up to no good.

Or, when he reads:

    ELSIE  (3,500 lbs.)

...he doesn't have to be told that Elsie resides somewhere in the Midwestern plains states, that she is a vegetarian, that she works outdoors, and that she has a peculiar fixation upon the moon, which will probably pay off in the final act, or later.

# SECTION 3:
# DIALOGUE

# III

Having grudgingly accepted the necessity of populating our screenplay with characters, we are heartened by the opportunity to give our characters something to say, thus making the best of a bad situation.

In Screenwriting 101, author Neil Hicks offers the following advice regarding how to write good dialogue: "Learn how to listen." Good Lord! What planet is this guy from? If this were the case, all that would be necessary to write good dialogue would be to watch (actually, hear) a lot of TV, or to have the radio turned on all day long. (Which, come to think of it, isn't such a bad idea after all; but let us not digress.) One need not engage in some Aristotelian flourish of convoluted logic to observe that to write good dialogue one must learn how to talk!

Fortunately, writers tend to be naturally gregarious and socially adept creatures, fluidly flitting from one topic to another as they make the social rounds. And these verbal skills turn the task of creating inspired dialogue into a walk in the park.

(Had we been able to cajole Mr. Hicks into writing a glowing review for this essay or offering us a reasonable cut of his obscene profits, we would have advised our readers to hurry out and buy his book, if only for the perverse pleasure of observing first-hand a real dilettante in action.)

## Writing Character-Specific Dialogue

It is often said that a reader should be able to distinguish one character from another merely by reading that character's dialogue, with the character's name blacked out, omitted or simply forgotten. This type of instruction, while possibly well intentioned, is naïve in the extreme, not to mention counterproductive and just plain mean-spirited.

After all, are we forgetting that the same writer wrote all the different characters' dialogue? Demanding that each character have a uniquely distinguishable voice is tantamount to asking the writer to wander off willy-nilly into disparate regions of his psyche, many of which are better off never seeing the light of day.

Additionally, we have already given our characters distinct names (we assume that none of our readers would be so stupid as to name one character "Rik" and another "Ri'ik"). And most screenwriting programs make it practically impossible to start writing dialogue without having first named the speaker.

And finally, let's not forget that we aren't writing "War and Peace" here; we're writing a screenplay, which will be performed by actual actors who, if the casting director has done his job and has not cast both Johnny Depp and Skeet Ulrich in the same picture, should not be too difficult for the audience to tell apart (same goes for Cameron Diaz, Angelina Jolie and Charlize Theron).

Despite these persuasive arguments, certain shrill, inordinately esteemed and overpaid pundits have succeeded in foisting their views upon their gullible sycophants. So, being pragmatic, we concede the necessity of making a token effort toward accommodating these nit-picking critics' juvenile sensibilities.

The solution is to write each character's dialogue in its own readily recognizable font.

Thus, when we read:

> (unnamed character #1)
> Fuck you!
>
> (unnamed character #2)
> **FUCK YOU!**
>
> (unnamed character #3)
> *Fuck you!*
>
> (unnamed character #4)
> ⟨alien script⟩

...we immediately know that the first line is spoken by our protagonist, Rik; the second is spoken by our antagonist, Ri'ik; the third is delivered by the romantic interest, Riki; and the fourth is the voice of our extraterrestrial alien, Rourke.

## Parentheticals

The latest idiotic trend in screenwriting is to limit the number of parentheticals (explicit directions to the actor) to a bare minimum. The theory behind this misguided imperative is that the actor will resent the screenwriter for telling him how to do his job (if you call acting a job).

But actors are fundamentally insecure, shallow and indolent beasts. And as such, they are always grateful for any and all direction you can provide them, so that they can spend less time in repetitive, tedious rehearsal and more time pursuing the script girl. So, be sure to throw in a plethora of these helpful directives, which will make the actor know you understand what he's up against and sympathize with his plight.

These lines:

                  ROK
     Fuck you!

...will engender terror in the poor actor, adrift in a sea of possible interpretations.

But, when the above line of dialogue is modified thus:

                  ROK
     (lights a cigarette with
     a chrome Zippo lighter)
  Fuck...
     (blows smoke ring;
     rolls his eyes)
  ...you...
     (a rasping cough,
     then hocks a loogie)
  ...!

...the actor will effortlessly deliver a perfect performance on the very first take.

A subtle variation is to give the actor only his emotional cues, without specifically identifying his physical actions. This approach has the advantage of maintaining the actor's childish illusion that his creativity is in any way involved in his performance:

>            ROK
> (with confidence, bordering
>    upon arrogance)
> Fuck...
>    (suddenly wracked by devastating
>    internal vacillation)
> ...you...
>    (with a cathartic burst of
>    deep resolve)
> ...!

Here, the actor will feel grounded and secure in his character's motivation, and will deliver a shattering performance, reeking of verisimilitude, laden with intimations of anonymous, urban angst.

Taking this principle to its logical extreme, we can combine the actor's physical and emotional cues, and reduce his dialogue accordingly:

>            ROK
> (with confidence, bordering
>    upon arrogance; lights a
>    cigarette with a chrome
>    Zippo lighter)
> ...
>    (suddenly wracked by devastating
>    internal vacillation; blows
>    smoke ring; rolls his eyes)

                    Dialogue | 51

                    ...
                        (with a cathartic burst of deep
                        resolve; a rasping cough,
                        then hocks a loogie)
                    ...!

Here, we are guaranteed a flawless physical interpretation, supported by subtly nuanced emotional underpinnings, with the added benefit that the actor need not even show up (or be paid) for his performance.

In fact, now we can write the scene exactly as it played in our mind's eye:

                            ROK
                        (with lights a confidence,
                        bordering cigarette with upon
                        a chrome arrogance; Zippo lighter)
                    ...
                        (suddenly blows wracked smoke
                        by ring; devastating rolls
                        internal his vacillation; eyes)
                    ...
                        (with a rasping cathartic cough,
                        burst then of hocks deep a
                        resolve; loogie)
                    ...!

We can practically visualize poor old Robert Towne, tearing out what remains of his hair after reading the virtuosic passage above.

## Writing the Star Vehicle

Getting a major star attached to your screenplay (not physically stapled to it, you dolt) is a sure-fire way to get the studios into a bidding war. So you must learn how to attract the interest of these peculiar creatures.

One accepted way to attract a specific movie star to your screenplay is to visualize that actor actually performing your character's action and delivering his dialogue. The downside is that you must spend endless hours trying to identify that actor's peculiar quirks, such as his taste in food, his favorite illegal drugs and his choice of defense attorneys (an actor who chooses Johnny Cochran is an entirely different animal from one who goes with, say, Spencer Tracy).

One solution is to simply give your character a name which is similar, if not identical, to the actor you are pursuing. For example, if we were writing the screenplay for Out of Sight, we would probably come up with a couple of character names like "J.Lo" and "Geo.Cloo."

But the sure-fire way to attract a major star to your screenplay is to write what is known as a "star vehicle," where they will be able to show off their subtle talents and demand the largest trailer on the set.

So, what distinguishes a star vehicle from another, less exalted role? In a word, inches. That's right, meathead, inches.

The first thing any actor does when he picks up your screenplay is to get out a ruler and add up all his character's lines of dialogue. When calculating his dialogue inches, the typical actor, known to be so mathematically inept as to be incapable of remembering his own age, suddenly becomes a mathematical wizard, as he effortlessly applies the following formula:

The typical 120-page screenplay has (assuming 1-inch top and bottom margins), at 9 inches of useable space per page, a total of 1080 inches available for typing. Since there should be a 2:1 correspondence between dialogue and exposition, that leaves a potential 720 inches for dialogue. Consequently, if your actor has at least 361 dialogue inches, there is a mathematical certainty that no other character can have more dialogue than he; he knows he has his hands on a star vehicle, and he is on the phone to his agent _now_.

# SECTION 4: EXPOSITION

# IV

The effective use of exposition will create in the reader a vivid visual image of the action that will take place on the screen. But the writer must perform a delicate balancing act, making sound judgements as to what constitutes essential description and what is merely superfluous detail.

See if you can determine what is wrong with the following expository passage:

```
Mattie's head, buried in a pillow, moving, her
body driven from behind.  Suddenly she turns
her face and she's looking right at us, her
expression serene for a moment, and then, just
as fast, contorted.  Tears.  She gasps.
```

First of all, is there some kind of sexual activity going on here? If so, quit beating around the bush and tell us. Now, we don't need to know such details as the precise coefficient of friction, or the specific gravity of the bodily fluids being exchanged, but we do need to know which orifices are involved, and in what order. (We are also curious about the sex of the participant(s).)

Most readers will admit, when threatened with a moistened cattle prod or a cervical fusion sans anaesthetic, that they occasionally skip right over your laboriously constructed exposition, slowing down to read only your dialogue. One way around this is to write exposition in **bold face**, <u>underlined</u> or in ALL CAPS, or by unexpectedly **changing fonts**. Some really eye-popping effects can be achieved by ComBJniNG tH eSE ELEMENts in delightfully unexpected ways.

It's a safe bet that this technique will stop even the most impatient reader dead in his tracks.

(Author's note: This section remains intentionally brief, in a magnanimous attempt to graphically convey to our less intellectually gifted readers the ever-increasing irrelevance of exposition in modern screenwriting.)

# SECTION 5:
# MOVIE TRIVIA QUIZ!

# V

Just for fun, let's give ourselves a breather from the dry, technical intricacies of screenwriting and take a little quiz, in which we will test our knowledge of the screenwriting craft and the movie business in general.

Your grades will not be recorded, and there is little likelihood you will fail. But if you should happen to answer one or more questions incorrectly, you might want to buy an additional 10 or 12 copies of this book and place them in strategic locations around your home, car and office, so you can take advantage of every spare opportunity to bone up on this important information.

## Screenwriting four Geniuses

1. What's wrong with the following quote from Scarface?

   > TONY MONTANA
   > Fock dos cockaroches, and fock de focking Diaz brothers.

   A. De wor "fock" ees meespelk
   B. De Diaz brothers not brothers, dey Vatos
   C. Chould bee sobtitle
   D. Ees poleetico eencorek

2. For extra credit, what movie is this quote from?

   A. Guys and Dolls
   B. Cinema Paradiso
   C. The Mexican
   D. 100 Years of Solitude

3. In <u>Evil Dead II</u>, who says the following line:

   > TONY MONTANA
   > Who's laughing now?

   A. Bruce Campbell
   B. Glen Campbell
   C. Naomi Campbell
   D. Sabine

4. Who put the "bomp" in the "whomp-alomp-abomp?"

   ☐ True
   ☐ False

Movie Trivia Quiz! 63

5. In <u>The Exorcist</u>, how do they get all that stuff to fly around the room like that?

    A. Wires
    B. Special Effects
    C. Too scary
    D. It's only a movie

6. Fill in the blanks. Write legibly.

    The _ itself.

7. Using a #2 pencil only, match the items on the left with the items on the right. The point of your pencil must never leave the page, and you must draw only perfectly straight lines, without any of the lines crossing. (Press firmly.)

| | |
|---|---|
| Alfred Hitchcock | Broad |
| Psycho | Movie |
| Janet Leigh | Director |
| Lee Atwater | |

8. What is your address, so I can come over and give you a piece of my mind?

    A. 1600 Pennsylvania Ave.

# SECTION 6:
# PROPER SCREENPLAY FORMAT

# VI

The proliferation of screenplay programs for computer makes it child's play to write a perfectly formatted screenplay, with proper margins, indenting and spacing. The problem now becomes how to stand out from the crowd, when one screenplay appears for all practical purposes indistinguishable from another.

## Get Visual, Already!

Since the purpose of a screenplay is to be translated into images which appear on the screen, the resourceful screenwriter pounces upon this golden opportunity to demonstrate his visual flair.

Therefore, be sure to decorate your screenplay with suggestive doodlings, or perhaps a collage of images to jog the reader's imagination into high gear. You may also sprinkle in judicious, candid photos of your younger sister and her friends, having been plied with some appropriately gooey liqueur and coerced into cavorting naked in the wading pool.

## Spelling

Serten werdz shud allwaze b speld fonetikle. (We're joking, of course. But we are confident that our fearless readers will forgive our brief excursion into levity, in the midst of this otherwise pedantic treatise. For they, better than most, recognize that we writers are natural-born raconteurs, ribald types always eager for an opportunity to rip off a knee-slapper.)

But there's more than a little truth behind this asershin. (There we go again!) The fact is, there is nothing you can do to undermine your career than to come off as some effete, holier-than-thou, pseudo-intellectual wise-ass, who can't resist rubbing the reader's nose in his own pitiful lack of imagination.

For example:

piqued, as in, "Her creamy white thighs piqued his interest..." - should be peaked, or - even better - peeked.

pored/pores, as in "Rodney pored over Eunice's will..." - use poured; or, "Her pores were like black, oily craters..." - write pours instead.

lode, as in "Clint, I think I've just shot the mother lode..." - always write load.

So, the astute reader is asking himself, where do we stop with this? What are the parameters governing when to bend the rules and when to stick to stodgy trudishn? (Stop us, before we jest again!) Well, this is strictly a judgement call, in which all of your creative instincts and artistic sensibilities are brought to bear. We assume of our readers certain discriminatory powers, a certain, shall we say, *raison d'être*, which will enable them to make the proper determination.

Bottom line, either you've got it or you don't. And the extent to which you insist upon holding us to some rigidly formulaic interpretation is probably a good indication that you would be better off seeking some less intuitive - and less profitable - line of work.

## Punctuation

In <u>Get Shorty</u>, the Hal Linden character, Bo Catlett, says not to worry about where all the commas go, because some proof reader at the studio will always add the punctuation for you later on. Our question is, if author James Ellroy is so smart, how come he writes these gooey novels instead of screenplays?

Forget about all that garbage you were taught in remedial English about how commas are used to separate compound phrases, or to separate items in a list. Here in Hollywood, commas are not grammatical devices, but are visual aids, the purpose of which is to enhance the telling of your story.

In our screenplay, commas are used to indicate a slight pause in the action, and should be inserted whenever the writer takes a puff of his cigarette. (If you are taking a longer break, such as to screw the Filipino houseboy, insert a paragraph break; for an extended departure, like entering rehab or undergoing elective cosmetic surgery to avoid detection by the IRS, insert a page break.)

Since screenplays are meant not to be merely read, but to be translated into faced-paced, high-voltage screen action, the ordinary period is to be avoided and replaced with the exclamation point. The standard texts agree upon the following convention: a single exclamation point is used to indicate a crisp, assertive ending, which serves to keep the reader on his toes; two represent a compact, muscular emphasis, which rivets the reader's attention to the page; and the effect of three exclamation points resembles a fiercely concentrated blow to the solar plexus, making the reader swoon with excitement, fall to his knees and cry out, "Yes!!!"

As usual, the candy-assed panty-waists who dispense this flaccid drivel fail to follow through upon a golden opportunity to inject real emotional vitality into your work. We humbly offer the following suggestion: Simply multiply the above quantities by a factor of roughly 3, thus coming up with !!!, !!!!!!, and, climactically, !!!!!!!!!.

Intersperse with other evocative, emotionally charged characters thus:

!?! - apparent finality, followed by momentary doubt, then a cathartic resolution

!?***?!? - the intimation of accord, immediately shattered by heart-rending angst

!!!!!!!*?!!! - seemingly unambiguous resolution, interrupted by a whiplash-like reversal, with a crescendo into orgiastic affirmation

!!!#%*++*?*!!@#!?*!"(?)"!!!© - here, the swirling emotional undercurrents and subtle cognitive atonality are practically impossible to comprehend

Regarding the colon, the semi-colon and the dash: Never - we repeat, never - use one of these pretentious, East-coast, Jewish liberal affectations in your screenplay; its presence will serve as a virtual magnet, ripping the manuscript out of your reader's hands and sucking it directly into the nearest circular file, where it goddamn well belongs.

Also avoid, as much as humanly possible, the use of parenthetical expressions. These pernicious grammatical entities, at once superfluous and ostentatious, serve only to alienate and enrage the reader. But, if you simply cannot refrain from proving to the world that you are a college-educated little prick, one who would be better suited to writing computer manuals for dyslexic, non-English-speaking, disadvantaged minorities, at least have the decency to never enclose parenthetical phrases within balanced commas, which only serve to accentuate their irrelevance to the issue at hand.

# SECTION 7:
# MISCELLANEOUS TRICKS
## of the TRADE

# VII

Such overpaid hacks as Mr. Hicks and Mr. McKee get a perverse kick out of bandying about such terms as "subtext" and "backstory," probably in the cynical expectation that their convoluted logic will prove so impenetrable that their readers will run out and buy another copy of their book, just to see if the latest edition contains any clarification or retraction.

## Subtext

The word "subtext" appears harmless at first glance. "Sub" means "under," and "text" means, well, "text." Under text. And what, exactly, is under text? Why, more text, of course. That is, unless the text itself is "FADE OUT," in which case what's under the text is blank space. So far, so good.

(The reader is cautioned that the hilarity induced by the following passage may lead to serious internal injury.)

But, according to these pundits, subtext has virtually nothing to do with text, period. Rather, they insist, the term relates to dialogue, and specifically refers to what the character is *not* saying while he is saying whatever it is he *is* saying (if anything).

As if this weren't enough, they go on to assert that this non-dialogue dialogue is in fact more important than the actual dialogue dialogue itself. And then, not content to merely controvert all norms of common sense, they go on to denigrate as "on the nose" all dialogue which has the temerity to actually say what it is saying, rather than the other way around.

Despite their argument's colossal stupidity and its blatant negation of logic - or perhaps because of it - these peripatetic purveyors of puerile perambulations have succeeded in ramming this ludicrous "subplot" criterion into the accepted lexicon of screenwriting criticism. But, being of good cheer, we shake our heads in resignation, while plotting the revenge we will inflict when we get around to detailing the use of plastic explosives to enhance the impact of query letters.

But if you are so congenitally spineless that you simply cannot refrain from indulging in this juvenile "subtext" nonsense, one solution is to use footnotes:

## Miscellaneous Tricks of the Trade 77

ROK
Screw you! (i)

.

.

.

(i) *Fuck you!*

This technique, reminiscent of that used in certain gynecological textbooks, is favored by academic types such as Michael Crichton.

(Inexplicably overcome by a spasm of creativity, we cannot restrain ourselves from launching into a terrific new story idea:

Mr. Crichton is a promising young physician named Danny DeVito, when in the midst of performing a delicate hypothalamic resection he experiences a sudden, tremendous growth spurt. Suddenly, the DeVito character molts right there in the operating theater into this gangly, new entity, the Crichton character, whose extraordinary size renders him unsuited to perform medicine. Kind of a Twins meets Dead Ringers. Let's see...Twin Ringers. No. How about Dead Twins? Even worse. Aha! Here we go: It's Twingers! And now, we imagine a sub-plot involving a pack of sex-crazed post-adolescents, driving all over the city trying to find a party, all the while trying and failing to speak with a lisp. Hilarity ensues.

In the devastating epilogue, we will reveal that the DeVito character has never been heard from since.)

Anyway, this footnote idea isn't too bad, especially considering that the whole "subtext" issue is a fraud, perpetrated by a bunch of pseudo-intellectual gangsters, cynically reveling in the prospect of making our lives miserable.

But what happens if you add a line of text <u>between</u> the footnote and the text to which it refers? Then, the footnote wraps around to the next page, and you're in a quandary, trying to figure out whether to delete some important earlier line, or to write 56 new lines to push the whole section onto the bottom of the next page. Or something like that.

One possible answer is the concept of *supratext* (™pending) in which the interpretation appears before the text it is interpreting:

(i)  *Fuck you!*

.

.

.

               ROK
       Screw you! (i)

By actually foreshadowing the dialogue with (what might eventually be) its hidden meaning, we thus introduce into our screenplay hitherto unimaginable new strata of lofty equivocation.

But suddenly, we realize we're once again stuck with that pesky problem of future inserted lines.

Perhaps the ideal solution is simply:

               ROK
      Screw you!
     *(Fuck you!)*

Or, write the subtext in a different color, exhale, and move on to a more pleasant activity.

## Subplots

If subtext in dialogue refers to what your character is not saying, then subplot in your story refers to what is not happening on screen.

But, while the concept of what is not being said is diabolically counter-intuitive, the idea of what is not happening is relatively easy to grasp and often makes a good deal of sense. Because, while there are only a finite number of things one can not say while simultaneously saying what one is saying, and - and here's the rub - having a good reason for not saying them, there are an almost unlimited number of things which are not happening while what is happening is happening, and virtually all of them have a perfectly reasonable explanation for why it is they are not happening (we won't belabor the elementary logic supporting this intuitively obvious assertion).

For example: Our protagonist is engaged in a no-holds-barred, mano a mano struggle with our antagonist. Just when it appears that our hero is done for, he reaches in and slowly rips our antagonist's liver out through his ass. It takes no great leap of logic to understand exactly why it is that, say, a group orgy is not happening. But the very fact that this group orgy is not happening serves to accentuate and enhance the inherent, irreverent humor and the riveting, unambiguous catharsis of the action on screen.

Now let's take a specific example from real life. In <u>Scarface,</u> (not the tedious, black-and-white documentary, but the Vittorio De Sica version starring Alan Pakula, of course), there is that classic scene where Tony Montana doesn't squish a grapefruit into (his future Mistress) Elvira's face. The fact that the filmmaker chose not to use a grapefruit, as opposed to not using an apple or, for that matter, a banana, serves to foreshadow and underscore the acidic quality which ultimately will not play a part in their emerging romantic relationship.

Clearly, the effective use of subplots is essential to the success of your screenplay. The better you understand and clearly delineate exactly what is not happening and precisely when it is not happening, the more successfully you will not convey this vital information to your audience.

## Backstory

"Backstory" is another one of those deliberately misleading terms concocted by the elite power structure to impede aspiring screenwriters from accomplishing their career goals, as they expend an inordinate amount of energy trying to find out where the space between the 2 words went.

Taken literally, "backstory" would seem to mean the tail end of your story, or possibly its reverse side. Or perhaps it is a term referring to the manner in which most females hanging around show biz moguls make their living.

But what "backstory" actually refers to is the action that has taken place <u>before</u> your actual screenplay begins (that they don't just call it "beforestory" is an indication of their devious mental process). Actually, the idea of "backstory" arose out of practical necessity: Somebody had to invent something that would enable them to avoid having to deal with these idiotic "psychological underpinnings" they came up with earlier on.

The pundits assert that the sublimely artistic method of introducing "backstory" (I, for one, am getting sick of this word, already, but *c'est la vie, c'est la guerre*) into your screenplay is to have it couched in dialogue, tucked away there in such an unobtrusive manner that the audience isn't aware it is being so cynically manipulated:

>                    ROK
>              (rolling his eyes)
>         Fuck...by the way, did I tell you
>         about the time my mother made my
>         puppy swallow furniture stripper and
>         then put him in the blender?...you!

As usual, these clowns are forgetting that we are writing for a visual medium here, not just for the unadulterated joy of spewing out a stream of 50-cent words, as in the little speech above.

Give us a flashback, for Pete's sake! Show us in living color that cuddly cocker spaniel being desiccated, diced and denuded while those whirring blades shriek in their high-pitched, migraine- inducing whine. Let us hear the puppy's plaintive yelping being slowly reduced to squishy gurgling, as he drowns in the liquefaction of his own internal organs.

Intercut with shots of adorable, 2-year-old Rok, lashed into his high chair with duct tape and being forced to watch the unfolding horror, his eyelids propped open with rusty, tetanus-laden carpet tacks.

Make us feel his pain!

## The "Beat" - Misunderstood, Misused and Mispronounced

When under pressure from any perceived challenge to their authority, seasoned Hollywood types are prone to casually sling around the term, "beat," knowing that doing so will engender in their rival a profound bewilderment, a free-floating, non-specific anxiety and a tremendous burning sensation in the genital area, while simultaneously inducing any heterosexual female of child-bearing age within a quarter-mile radius to swoon and start ripping off her clothes in a frenzy of sexual abandon.

"Beat" is an inherently - *je ne sais quoi* - indefinable, self-referential expression, so insular and laden with metaphysical connotations known only to the *cognoscenti* that any further attempt to clarify it *a priori* must fall *de facto* upon deaf ears, *e pluribus unum*. If pressed to provide an explanation, we might deign to proffer that the term "beat" is used to connote a hermetically discrete, supranormal, recursive narrative entity, the definition of which is the word "beat."

Another commonly held, yet demonstrably preposterous, interpretation is that "beat" is used to indicate a pause in a character's dialogue.

See if you can identify what's wrong with the following example, in which the misguided writer attempts to insert a pregnant pause into the protagonist's heart-wrenching soliloquy:

```
               ROK
     Fuck
                (beat)
     you.
```

If you answered, "You shouldn't direct the actor," you would be not only wrong, but also certifiably criminally insane. The (what we assumed to be self-evident) point is that "beat" should never be used in dialogue, period.

The above example should be written:

>                    ROK
>           Fuck
>
>
>
>           you.

Here, the blank space doesn't merely convey the idea of a pause, it is a pause in and of itself. Never forget, you thick-headed imbecile, that film is a visual medium; until you get this rudimentary principle through your bovine skull, you deserve to spend every miserable minute and more of what's left of your puny, insignificant existence at that $6.25 McJob of yours, slinging hash for the serial rapists at the local greasy spoon.

(If we sound a tad snippy, imagine how you would feel if you were us, constantly beset by packs of waddling, Midwestern Protestants, wielding Kodak Instamatics and clad in tank-tops, bermuda shorts and Rockports, shrilly imploring you to impart just one more teensy facet of your hard-earned superciliousness, to be oh-so-reverentially dispensed to their cretinous, inbred offspring back home in Des Moines.)

## Product Placement

It is well known that filmmakers receive extraordinary sums of money to insert brand-name products in their films. That single can of Coke you see being guzzled by Our Hero, after having graphically disemboweled the 18 ninjas surrounding him with a rusty, $2.95 box-cutter, probably represents a brand new, 50-meter, black-bottomed pool in the director's back yard and a shiny, new BMW 330ci in his mistress's garage.

What is less widely known is that screenwriters are also the recipients of the multinational corporations' largesse.

Thus, your screenplay's Dutiful Wife doesn't just pour out a bowl of cornflakes for her adorable, tow-headed identical Twins, but gives them "New, Improved, Super-Crinkly Kellogg's/Mobil Oil Enhanced Flakeoids© with All Natural Sun Microsystems Carnuba Oil®." Then, just sit back and wait for your 6-figure fee, and all this for only a few moments' typing.

Peppering your screenplay with product references and brand names also conveys a sense of authenticity, demonstrating your intimacy with your story elements and your comprehensive vision of the world you have created. Plus, it engenders in the reader a warm and fuzzy familiarity, a kind of beatific retardation, in which he forgets that he is slogging through a voluminous, 120-page opus, but rather feels as if he were being whisked through a fast-paced montage of his favorite TV commercials.

And this observation leads us seamlessly to our next exciting topic.

# SECTION 8:
# WRITING *for* TELEVISION

# VIII

Preposterous as this may seem, there actually is a bit of snobbery in Hollywood, and the mere mention of television is often sufficient for it to rear its ugly head. For some inexplicable reason, television is perceived as smaller, thicker and tinnier than its wide-screen equivalent. To perpetuate these stereotypes, cineastic types often throw around such supposedly derogatory technical phrases as "aspect ratio," "pan and scan" and "new and improved."

But, if you are fortunate enough to possess a sunny, uncritical disposition, a naturally short attention span and an inclination to laugh at the merest intimation of humor (such as a canned laugh track), then you are probably an excellent candidate to participate in this extraordinarily lucrative and intellectually non-invasive medium.

Movies, by virtue of their unwieldy size, outsized budgets, lengthy running times and occasionally lethal decibel levels, are limited to a few tried-and-true genres. By contrast, television, with its proliferation of niches, micro-niches and combi-niches, offers an almost infinite variety of opportunities for the ambitious writer to flourish.

There are sitcoms, docudramas, infomercials, 256 different types of cop shows, 88 courtroom drams, soft-core porn, women-themed shows, gay-themed shows, cooking shows, non-stop news, trash news, non-stop trash news, non-stop trash non-news, African-American-themed shows (the NBA), Cuban-themed shows (baseball, which by the way is not a sport; despite the protestations of a certain reactionary commentator working on the early Sunday Morning ABC news/talk/celebrity show, and bearing a more than passing physical and psychological resemblance to Adolf Hitler, baseball barely qualifies as even an "activity"), trash sports, Euro-trash sports, talk shows, talk shows, talk shows, dog shows, dog and pony shows, and murky, pseudo-science fiction shows conceived, written and filmed entirely in the absence of light.

There is television for homosexuals ("Queer as Folk"), television for geriatrics ("Diagnosis Murder"), television for amateur sleuths and aspiring small-time criminals ("Unsolved Mysteries"), television for spastic animals and their retarded owners ("That Stupid Pet Show"), television for ordinary spastics (the XFL - oh, well), television for artsy-fartsy liberals (PBS), television for women over 35 with the emotional maturity of 13-year-olds ("Sex and the City")...and we're just getting started!

Let's take a look at just how many different varieties of program can appear in one of these tiny niches, Lifetime Network ("Television For Women," for God's sake!): We've got husbands killing wives, husbands killing daughters, husbands raping wives, husbands raping daughters, husbands killing wives and raping daughters, husbands killing daughters and raping wives, boyfriends killing and raping...you get our drift. (No, we haven't forgotten that Lifetime stalwart, women killing other women. But why the dumb broads producing these shows don't realize that what we really want is women raping and killing other women is a mystery to us.)

And the really great thing, from the writer's point of view, is that every one of these shows actually consists of only 1.75 minutes of actual show per half-hour of running time, the remaining 16.66 minutes being occupied by sponsor-supplied commercials. (There are those cynical observers who claim that all the shows on television exist solely for the sponsors to have an opportunity to hawk their products! We will respond only by pointing out that if this were the case, how do these same cynics explain the classic writing, acting and groundbreaking story lines of such unforgettable TV shows as that one with the Martian, and that other one with the lesbian?)

On account of these miniscule actual program durations, the typical TV writer works less than half an hour a day. Aaron Sorkin, the visionary credited with the revolutionary, time-saving concept of having every character's dialogue be identical to every other character's dialogue, has been known to churn out 2 complete shows a week while working less than 4 minutes a day, leaving the remaining 15-plus hours to smoke crack, eat mushrooms, joy-ride all over Burbank in Jay Leno's Bugatti, chase the script girl around the commissary, and still have time left over to tearfully apologize to the rest of us (through his personal assistant).

In short, network television is an ideal respite for any writer whose "f," "u," "c" and "k" keys have been ground down to fine dust, or whose incessant screwing of young starlets has given him carpal tunnel syndrome of the hip flexors, or who has simply run out of ideas.

# SECTION 9:
# ASK *the* EXPERT!

# IX

In this section, we will attempt to answer some of the questions we have received over the years from our readers, from bright-eyed, bushy-tailed, novice screenwriters eager to get their foot in the door, to hardened professionals trying like the dickens to get their foot back out again.

Q: *I have written a comedy/thriller screenplay that is so timely and so high-concept that I'm afraid to show it to just anyone, for fear I'll get ripped off. What should I do? S.B. - Montecito, CA*

A: Before you send a copy to those socialist dogs at the Writers Guild or to those underpaid, thieving bureaucrats at the copyright office, send a copy directly to the author (the author's personal assistant). He (the author's personal assistant) will read it carefully and get back to you immediately or sooner, whichever comes later.

Q: I'm thinking of starting off my screenplay like this:

FADE IN:

Flames in a night sky.

What do you think? - L.K., Los Angeles, CA

A: Regrettably, it would appear you are a novelist. Kindly refrain from ever contacting us again.

Q: William Goldman says that nobody in Hollywood knows anything. What makes you think you're any different? - R.S., Santa Monica, CA

A: If you had the minimum complement of functioning synapses required to parse Mr. Goldman's thinly disguised double-negative, you would come up with, "Everybody in Hollywood knows everything." Now, shut your wise-ass mouth and bring us our latte.

Q: Everybody says that you have to have an agent to sell a screenplay. But to get an agent, first you have to sell a screenplay. This sounds like a Catch-22 to me. - J.H., Cincinnati, OH

A: Had you actually seen the Robert Altman film to which you are apparently referring, you would have realized that it has absolutely nothing to do with selling a screenplay or getting an agent. But you had us going for a minute there.

Q: How do you handle plot holes? - S.F., Venice, CA

A: With great care! Seriously, though, the handling of holes of any kind is a delicate matter, best left to professionals with the appropriate outer wear and all-terrain vehicles.

Q: How do you deal with ageism in Hollywood? Specifically, I'm a 42-year-ol-- J.C., Des Moines, IO

A: Hold it right there, Fella. Sorry to so rudely interrupt, but we do have our serious readers, and we don't want to waste their valuable time with frivolous questions from a bunch of addled, over-the-hill geezers who couldn't write a fart joke if it came up and bit them on the ass. All we can say is, better hang onto your day job, or, better yet, just blow your brains out while you still have the mental capacity to make such arrangements.

Q: I'm a 19-year-old female beauty queen, eager to write a screenplay about my experiences as a high-fashion model and porn star. Where do I start? - Debbie, Dallas, TX

A: Immediately get on the next plane to L.A., and see us for a personal consultation.

# SECTION 10:
# LET'S GET *to* WORK!

# X

**O**K! We've mastered all the fundamentals, and we're champing at the bit to churn out the first installment of our franchise. How do we begin our screenplay? It's crucial that we start with a slam-bang opening, one which rivets the reader to the page.

## Getting Started

Fortunately, the etiquette of screenplay format provides us with an automatic, can't-miss formula for getting over this obstacle, which has caused many potential novelists, poets and obituary writers to abandon hope.

With a flourish, we write:

> FADE IN:

...and our mind goes blank. An insidious terror permeates our consciousness, we break into a clammy sweat and we begin to sink into despair. Our mind starts playing tricks on us: We calculate that we have written one single line, and that, at 56 lines per page and 120 pages per screenplay, there are 119 pages and 55 lines left before we're done; doing the math, we realize that we're only 1/6720$^{th}$ of the way to the end. Our spirits are somewhat buoyed when we realize that there is a blank line after "FADE IN:," meaning we're actually 1/3360$^{th}$ of the way there. But still...this isn't as easy as we thought!

If only we could get to "FADE OUT!" Then, even if we've written a lifeless, incoherent piece of dreck that is probably destined to become merely a routine HBO miniseries, we'll at least have something to work with, something to mold into our masterpiece.

A time-tested way over the hump is to write:

> FADE IN:
>
> FADE OUT

...and then just fill in the stuff in between. In less than 12 seconds, you have written an entire screenplay, from beginning to end, lacking only some rhetorical puffery to occupy the middle section. (Be sure to have "Insert" activated on your computer when you employ this technique, or you will defeat yourself in a matter of seconds.)

## The Pharmacology of Inspiration

For hyper-analytical anal retentives, or for those who are so immobilized by societal injunctions against spontaneity that they are incapable of grasping the childishly simple solution delineated in the section above, there are other techniques we can bring to bear to make the process easier.

Writers throughout the ages have used a variety of natural and artificial stimulants, depressants, hallucinogens, hypnotics, industrial solvents and assorted methane-based explosives to jog their imaginations into high gear. Plus, it is a proven career booster for the writer to have at least a rudimentary working knowledge of these substances; with a little luck, this experimentation will result in full-blown addiction, which will enable him to enter rehab or attend AA, NA or CA meetings - where most Hollywood business relationships, marriages and extra-marital affairs are initiated - without arousing suspicion that he is a DEA informant, or, God forbid, a musician.

(For those impassioned, ultra-committed screenwriters for whom mere billions of dollars and the envy of mankind is simply not enough, a heavy Jones opens up the perfect opportunity to make the ultimate career move: premature death.)

Before launching into any program of unsupervised pharmacological experimentation, you must take certain steps to prepare your nervous system, much as a professional athlete goes into training before a big match.

First off, if you don't smoke, start immediately. If you already smoke, move to the non-filters. And get yourself one of those flip-top Zippo-type lighters right away, to familiarize yourself with the workings of this essential film prop. (As you know, all characters in your screenplay must smoke, and any discriminating reader will be able to spot in an instant any hint of inauthenticity on your part. The use of a butane lighter is a career-ender.)

Next, get yourself a case of hard liquor, preferably 100-proof. Start off by putting a couple of ounces in your coffee (or on your cereal) in the morning, and as quickly as possible increase the ratio until you're knocking back (or lapping up) the pure spirits.

After about a month, your body will be ready to endure the withering demands you will place upon it, as you learn to mix and match to achieve precisely the correct balance of inspiration, disorientation and recklessness appropriate to the writing of any particular scene.

Here is a brief guide to the particular writing obstacles these substances will help you to overcome:

(Rest assured that your intrepid Author, being pure as the driven snow, comes by this information in a purely anecdotal manner.)

*Marijuana.* Essential for all comedy writing. Pot is well known to cause the "laughies," where the user perceives everything to be funnier than it actually is; what is lesser known is that it actually makes the user himself much funnier than he actually is. Also good for meandering, amorphous "stream of unconsciousness" passages, where one wishes to impart a sense of focused indecision.

*Methamphetamines.* Good for convoluted, recursive dialogue, serpentine plotting and for writing in extremely small fonts.

*Psychedelics.* Good for florid exposition, wishy-washy, mystical self-revelation and for doodling on the cover and in the margins. Good for gay or feminist-tinged, "inclusive" nonsense.

*Coffee.* Good only for writing for television.

*Barbiturates.* Good for multi-vehicle car crashes, barroom

Let's Get to Work! | 105

fig. 64-b

brawls and for writing in authentic southern drawls. Also useful for writing in black and white.

*Cocaine.* Excellent for imparting authentic, urban angst. Good for scenes involving tunneling into bank vaults. Helpful for scenes showing intense sexual obsession and for scenes portraying bleeding of the internal organs.

*Opiates.* Good for lugubrious, Merchant/Ivory-type affairs, where the viewer can go into the kitchen, wolf down a sandwich with all the fixins, come back into the living room, sit down for the movie and feel an instantaneous need to repeat this entire process. Excellent for writing in an undecipherable English accent.

*Alcohol.* Good for everything.

*More Alcohol.* Good for everything else.

## Get Out of That Rut

Occasionally, even with the aid of the substances mentioned above, a seasoned writer gets stuck. It is difficult for the common man - the "regular Joe," the stupefyingly ordinary working stiff, unburdened as he is by any shred of the talent, intelligence or imagination necessary to escape the bone-crushing tedium of his repetitive, meaningless existence - to comprehend the discomfort the writer experiences when faced with a momentary absence of ideas.

But, for the creatively gifted, filthy rich and sexually fulfilled screenwriter, a jaunt to the local, triple-priced specialty market to stock up on the day's supply of Beluga caviar and Dom Perignon is often all that's needed to jog his creativity and imagination into high gear.

Strolling down the canned vegetable aisle, we spot a can of kidney beans. Hmmm, we reason. Kidney beans...kidneys...We all know how much it hurts to get whacked in the kidneys with a red-hot tire iron. Aha! What we need is a fight scene! Even the clotted, scarlet hue of those kidney beans suggests the horrific violence with which we will imbue this titanic clash.

Now, stroll along the meats section. Look at those chicken breasts. Let's see...chicken breasts...chicken...Our hero is waffling, unable to decide whether to run or to fight! What's needed is to delve into his inner conflicts, to probe his nagging doubts about the function of masculinity in our post-feminist society (actually, it would appear we were thinking not about our hero, but rather about our moustache-twirling antagonist here). Peeling away layer after layer of latent meaning, we proceed to explore just how we will best portray this riveting pathos: Chicken breasts...breasts... *Sacre bleu!* With a flood of Freudian insight, we trace these feelings of inadequacy back to his tumultuous relationship with his domineering mother! We will use a flashback, in which his mother humiliates his sniveling father with a rhinestone-encrusted riding crop, right in front of her Thursday night, lesbian biker bridge club.

Now, we're in the fruits and vegetables section. Those artichokes...well, aside from their obvious sexual connotations, it's a little hard to get a fix on what they are telling us. Perhaps we were thinking of asparagus.

But at this point, our crisis of confidence is over. Without having spent a dime or consumed a single empty calorie, we are back on track, ready to tackle any obstacle.

# Begging, Borrowing and Your 1ST Amendment Rights

If imitation is the sincerest form of flattery, then plagiarism is the expression of unrestrained adoration. Remember, screenwriters are human after all, and they appreciate being acknowledged by their peers and admirers just like the rest of us. Bottom line, successful screenwriters are really no different from the rest of us, except that they are rich and happy.

Stories abound of writers, highly compensated professionals as well as lowly beginners, submitting works which are brazenly stolen from others, with merely the title changed and a few extra explosions, dismemberments and exclamation points inserted. For an indication of how prevalent this phenomenon is, merely observe that L.A. Confidential is actually Chinatown, only with the voice-over replaced by subtitles; and, further, note that every Michael Bay movie is in every detail indistinguishable from every other Michael Bay movie. (Plagiarizing from yourself takes flattery, hero worship and self-love to dizzying new heights.)

One such story from the arcane literary world - a world the serious screenwriter should avoid like a case of slow stomach cancer - is that some demented, aspiring novelist (is there any other kind?) re-typed the award-winning Theodore Kaczynski novel, The Painted Bird, gave it a new title and submitted it to a dozen or so publishers, among them the actual publisher of the original book. Needless to say, none of these publishers even recognized the deception; the supposed jaw-dropping capper is that every one of them, including the original publisher, gave it a "Pass." Now, some wise-ass reader is probably assuming that the real punchline is that this pretentious piece of dreck was ever written, published or even read in the first place. But the actual kicker - and this is a considerably less comforting observation - is that our current, enlightened Judiciary permits this filthy, verbose and effeminate art form to continue to exist at all.

But even if someone were to notice that your material has been "borrowed," the point is that in the self-referential world of Hollywood, plagiarism is regarded not as intellectual thievery, but rather as homage. In meticulously recreating every subtle nuance of the work he is honoring, the filmmaker is acknowledging the artistic groundwork laid by those pioneers who came before him, who lifted the idea from their predecessors in a similar magnanimous gesture. This demonstration of generosity and obeisance also relieves the writer, director and actors of forever having to concoct new and untested ideas, which usually accomplish little more than mystify the unimaginative cretins who make up the movie-going audience.

The issuing of sequels, prequels, in-between-quels, knock-offs, rip-offs and jack-offs reassures the viewer that he will not be coughing up $9.50 a ticket (not counting parking, popcorn, prophylactics and subsequent visits to the local ear, nose and throat specialist) to be a guinea pig for some snotty *artiste* with a "refreshing and original" (read: muddled and pretentious) take on life. Hell, for all we know, this guy has some cockamamie idea about a dysfunctional suburban family whose father quits his job, starts listening to rock-and-roll and goes to work at a fast-food joint; or about some dead psychologist who doesn't even realize he's dead.

As an added incentive to assuage the doubts of our more squeamish readers, rumor has it that the current Cheney/Scalia Administration is considering eliminating all corporate restrictions on the use, re-use, duplication and mutilation of intellectual property, in the interests of enhanced interstate commerce and unimpeded capital aggregation.

Now, if they could just do something about that Bolshevik concept, "intellectual property."

# SECTION 11:
# PLAYING *the* HOLLYWOOD GAME – *and* KICKING SERIOUS BUTT!

# XI

Just writing a great screenplay isn't enough. You must have a practical understanding of the Hollywood hierarchy and an insight into its peculiar operating methods to really make it big.

## Getting Past the Professional Reader

All executives at production companies, literary agencies and movie studios employ professional readers to pick up their dry cleaning, provide them with sexual favors and, occasionally, read a script and provide an analysis. Owing to her being the first line of resistance through which all aspiring screenwriters must pass, yet destined herself to never attaining anything of value, the Reader has the dubious distinction of being at once the single most indispensable and simultaneously the most universally reviled creature in the Hollywood food chain.

It is crucial to remember that the Reader hates you and wants you to fail. So, it is in your best interest to understand the Reader's unique combination of meager assets and crippling liabilities, so that you may exploit these to your advantage.

The typical Reader is a female in her early 20s, and is armed with a bachelor's degree in English, which she had hoped would provide her with the perfect entrée into the upper echelons of the movie business. But, having been unaware that the ability to read is considered a detriment in Hollywood, the Reader is now prematurely bitter, her colossal student loans forever reminding her that it is precisely her expensive education which will prevent her from ever advancing up the career ladder.

The Reader is often burdened by some physical deformity, such as one leg being shorter than the other, or a wandering eyeball. No matter how much effort she puts into her wardrobe, her clothes seem to hang upon her awkwardly, and she may emit a foul odor.

The concluding section of the Reader's script analysis is a rating, which consists of either a "Recommend," a "Consider" or a "Pass." Your goal is to get that "Recommend," come hell or high water.

Should the Reader give a "Recommend" rating, her boss will

immediately fork over an exorbitant sum of money to obtain this property. And then, if it subsequently fails to generate at least $100 million domestic, neither the Reader nor any member of her immediate or extended family will work, or be capable of working, ever again. Consequently, any reader who has been around for longer than 2 weeks knows to never give out this rating. Indeed, her very life and the lives of all those close to her are entirely dependent upon her issuing one "Pass" after another.

(Not only does this practice provide her with job security, it relieves her of the responsibility of having to even lightly skim anything sent her way. Experienced readers can thus "read" up to 100 scripts and 50 books per week, and, at up to $5.00 a crack, well, you do the math.)

The most straightforward way to get a "Recommend" rating from a Reader is to clip a $50 bill directly to your screenplay (specifically, to the last page; this is the first - indeed, often the only - page the Reader will look at). This way, the Reader knows that you sympathize with her plight and that you know how to play the Hollywood game. If you're in a jocular mood, you might also attach a note stating that you know her address, and that you would be delighted to drop by unannounced to provide her with some outcall reconstructive dental work, or perhaps an impromptu rhinoplasty.

## Getting an Agent

If the studio Reader is the most detested creature in the Hollywood system, the Agent is the most adored and revered.

In most respects, the Agent is the polar opposite of the Reader: The Agent is a 30-year-old, white male, a junior-high school dropout who cannot read a cashier's check without moving his lips. He can neither read, write, sing, dance, act, play an instrument, listen, hear, see, jump nor rhyme. Yet despite this litany of apparent liabilities - or perhaps because of it - the Agent possesses an uncanny, predatory ability to seek out whatever miniscule shred of veracity may be present in any situation and instantaneously cause it to vanish into thin air.

In fact, the Agent's most highly developed talent is for talking on the telephone. Such is his affinity for this instrument that whenever a conversation veers perilously close to specifics, the nearest telephone immediately starts to ring, sometimes leaping into the Agent's hand and occasionally actually affixing itself directly onto the Agent's ear.

The Agent is a skittish, aquiline creature with a distinctly rodent-like appearance. His eyes are beady and close together, and, despite his notoriously fragile jaw, his teeth are especially suited to gnawing. His face is frozen into a skeletal, insincere smile, an affectation that is magnified when he senses he is being scrutinized. He possesses tremendous quantities of nervous energy, which may be due to the copious quantities of coffee, methamphetamines and cocaine he consumes.

One should eschew coming within close proximity to the Agent, and actual physical contact is to be avoided at all costs, as the Agent's pores secrete an oily, acidic residue which has been known to cause blindness, sterility and a shriveling (or vanishing) of the cerebral cortex.

One of the Agent's glaring weaknesses, aside from his lack of any discernible judgement, intelligence, talent, creativity, vision, wisdom, courage or conviction, is his oversized ego. He will never fail to respond positively to your telling him you couldn't have done it without him, or that without him you are nothing, or that your most fervent desire is to be just like him, or - better yet - to actually *be* him. Possibly because of his conspicuous dearth of muscle tissue, hand-eye coordination and athletic ability, the Agent is delighted to be told that you fear him.

But perhaps his most pathetically transparent vulnerability is the Agent's belief that he can write. Believe it or not, he often sincerely believes that he himself has written your screenplay, or, even if he doesn't actually believe this, he will nevertheless go right ahead and tell everyone else that this is the case. Consequently, an especially effective way to win him over is, when you mail him your screenplay, to include a letter congratulating him for the phenomenal screenplay he has just written.

Above all, never forget that the Agent, accustomed as he is to constantly dispensing hyperbolae, evasions, obfuscations, exaggerations, contradictions, gibberish, non-sequiters and bald-faced lies, similarly expects always to be lied to. Should he ever ascertain that you have told him the truth, he will destroy you.

## Development Heaven

Wow! You now have an agent, and you have also made your first sale! (At the risk of sounding repetitive, for the benefit of our analytically challenged readers we state the truism: You couldn't sell anything until you got an agent, and you couldn't get an agent until you sold something. Ergo, you sold something. Repeat as necessary.)

So now it's time for your first meeting with the studio bigwigs, and you're a little nervous! What if they don't like you? What should you wear? What if they want to turn your "baby," with all its galaxy-shredding super-novae and white-hot lesbian sex, into some lugubrious period piece, where Kenneth Branagh and Emma Thompson mope around in tutus, mumbling in unintelligible, phony British accents about how the play's the thing?

Well, you can just relax and stop worrying. These development execs need you and love you more than you will ever know! After all, you are the writer, without whom all those glorious movies would never exist in the first place. It's their job to help you realize your vision, and they will do everything in their power to accommodate you and to make your task easier. When the studio head played by Michael Landon in <u>Barton Fink</u> says the writer is king in this business, he means business!

In fact, these people are actually more frightened of you than you are of them. They know that their jobs are on the line here, and that if any word should filter back to the tough, no-nonsense, cigar-chomping studio boss that they have in any way offended you, they will be on the next bus back to Fresno, probably in separate suitcases.

An excellent way to "break the ice" on your first meeting is to subtly make known your sexual availability to the female members of your team. Start with the receptionist, who is really scared and in need of reassurance, as she has been hired entirely on the basis of her 8- by 10-inch glossy, certainly not for her intelligence or her clerical skills. As she ushers you into the meeting, give her a firm, probing caress deep up the glorious crack of her incredibly toned ass (my God, you'll swear, I'll bet she can crack walnuts with that thing!).

Be sure to take a seat next to the most attractive female member of the team, and, as you take your seat, under the pretense of whispering a personal greeting, surreptitiously ram your tongue into her ear and give it a vigorous flutter. The first time she offers a creative suggestion, slide your hand up her silky inner thigh towards her crotch, thrust her panties aside, and...we leave the rest to your lusty imagination.

The trick to winning over the male members of the team is to keep them appropriately cowed, without stepping over the line and causing them to actually break into tears. One disarmingly effective technique is to "accidentally" forget their names, or to get them confused with each other.

Remember, from this day forward you will never again merely "go to" a meeting, you will "take" a meeting. Seen in this light, the transformation your life has undergone is awesome indeed. Never again will you have to "get" a haircut, "have" lunch, "get" laid or "play" a round of golf; from now on, you will just "take" everything. It's just take, take, take, all the way to the bank!

# SECTION 12:
# BEYOND SUCCESS

# XII

It's been an arduous, 6- to 9-week process, but your efforts have paid off in spades. And now, it is perfectly understandable that you might want to sit back and bask in the glow of your accomplishments.

You must resist such temptation. There is nothing so despicable as achieving great success and then demonstrating contempt for that very success by refusing to flaunt it in as conspicuous and ostentatious a manner as possible. Never forget that there are legions of potential rivals brawling down there in the muck, seeking to deprive you of your exalted status. You have a responsibility to give these imposters on the horizon something to envy and to strive for, and at the same time make their task as close to impossible as you can.

When it comes to the exercise of power, Hollywood has some delightfully quaint and idiosyncratic customs, which might seem peculiar to the uninitiated, but which will become second nature with a bit of practice.

It is a well-known truism that power flows down, never up. What is lesser known is that this power, like a heavy object falling from the sky at the rate of 30 feet per second per second, increases in both its strength and its absence of logic as it progresses downward.

Thus, a mid-level executive on the receiving end of the CEO's abuse of power might receive some mild rebuke, such as having his identity stolen and his credit rating destroyed, while a clerk in the mail room who happens to be in the wrong place at the wrong time will be fortunate to get off with so light a penalty as public castration and the appropriation of his entire family into indentured servitude.

This runs contrary to the supposedly more mature view that true satisfaction derives from besting one's equal or one's superior, and that there is little satisfaction to be gained by pounding upon some insignificant weakling, who presumably is already suffering more than is absolutely necessary.

But here in Hollywood, while we live in a world of dreams, in which our inner child is given free rein of expression, we are also pragmatists. Thus, we only pick fights we are absolutely certain of winning. And belting our helpless inferiors in the teeth, behavior which elsewhere would be viewed as a demonstration of unconscionable immaturity, is rightfully seen as our being in touch with our unsullied, childlike emotions.

So, kick that cripple! Humiliate that word processor! Be a man!

Beyond Success | 125

## Giving Back to the Community - In Spades

It is a sad truth that there will be those who will envy you and resent your success, and will even wish you ill. Your occasional, meticulously calculated spontaneous display of generosity goes a long way toward enhancing your status as a pillar of the community, while simultaneously gently poking fun at these self-righteous malcontents' shortsightedness.

So, let's give our creative fervor free rein, as we construct a hypothetical scenario with the same effortlessness with which we compose a 22-vehicle car crash or a homosexual gang rape:

*In the dim recesses of your memory, you happen to recall your old chums from the office pool, and, as if out of the ether, a plan congeals in your fertile imagination. You have your personal assistant call up 10 or 12 of them, and invite them to meet you for dinner at one of the most exclusive restaurants in town. Expense is no object, you (through your assistant) assure them. But, you regretfully add, this establishment does enforce a strict dress code.*

*You arrive a fashionable 90 minutes late, wearing jeans and a (clean) white t-shirt. No, you didn't have to grease the maitre'd, you confess to your overdressed pals with a laugh - they know you here, and they are accustomed to supplicating themselves before the every whim of the artistic temperament.*

*You sit down and, without so much as glancing at the wine list, order a dozen bottles of Dom Perignon '85, a similar quantity of '92 Echezeaux, and, in a flamboyant nod to moderation, one mere magnum of Chateau d'Yquem '75. You share an inside joke - in adequate French - with the wine steward, then apologize to your overdressed friends for your rusty accent, not having been on the Continent for over*

*6 weeks. You order the chateaubriand and Alaskan king crab for 2 for each of your pals, waving off their flimsy protestations with a breezy jocularity.*

*Throughout the sumptuous meal, you regale your now thoroughly enthralled audience with ever-more hilarious tales of the riotous foibles of the super-elite. Your magnanimity is in full evidence, as you deny them even a moment's indulgence to discuss some depressing war in some impoverished, 3$^{rd}$ world backwater, or to describe some tedious fiduciary triviality impinging upon their own mundane world. You're here to forget all that!*

*An awkwardness threatens to invade your camaraderie, however, when Clem, his lower lip quavering tremulously, describes in excruciatingly embarrassing detail how his HMO is refusing to cover an experimental surgical procedure necessary to save the life of his ailing, 3-year-old daughter. It seems little Jodie suffers from a rare and debilitating chemical imbalance which renders her incapable of receiving love, leaving her emaciated, bewildered and hopelessly alone.*

*An adolescent squeal emanating from the front door conveniently interrupts Clem's litany of woe, as Pamela Anderson Lee spots you and breathlessly rushes to your side.*

*Doggedly, Clem goes on to say that he has taken out a 3$^{rd}$ mortgage (whatever that is) at 19.9 percent on his 800-square-foot Pomona tract home, the one with the '88 Hyundai Excel in the driveway, the window box containing a plot of herbs, which, despite constant, loving attention struggles vainly against the stifling heat and the oppressive smog, and on the front doorstep the welcome mat, hand-embroidered with the inscription,* **"God Bless Our Happy Home."** *Despite your adroitly contrived embarrassment,*

Pamela proceeds to smother you with wet kisses, all the while cooing about how much she has missed you, and why couldn't you just call her once in a while?

Just as Clem reaches into his pocket and retrieves his wallet, packed with a 1-inch-thick stack of credit cards, and thrusts out a snapshot of the adorably pathetic toddler, the teary-eyed Pamela utters a sob of unrestrained joy, hurls herself beneath the table and proceeds to have her way with you.

Forlornly staring up at you from the dog-eared snapshot, the doomed little Jodie, in her scrupulously patched and crisply pressed gingham dress, with her Walter Keane-like eyes wide as a pair of saucers, is beginning to arouse your sympathy. But then, Pamela's silky hands and her pouty lips cause your eyes to involuntarily glaze over.

Wiping away a tear, with a trembling finger Clem points out Jodie's hand-hewn, pine leg braces with their shiny hinges, the proceeds for which were raised at a bake sale put on by the PTA down at the local Methodist church. But you are having a really difficult time concentrating, as Pamela's tongue is now rooting around somewhere up near your esophagus. A blubbery, lower-middle-class wail wafts into your consciousness, and you remotely sense Clem lurching out of his chair and bolting toward the men's room. The last thing you recall, just before your consciousness is subsumed by an earth-shattering orgasm, is the crack of Clem's corpulent ass, packed lumpily into what you are mortified to observe is a pair of rumpled, black Dockers, so poorly concealed beneath his ill-fitting, rented tuxedo.

When the check arrives, your friends, being well-domesticated by their domineering, thick-legged significant others, will no doubt reach for their wallets. But you insist - no, *demand! - that you pick up the tab. It's tax deductible, after all, and...But, sacre bleu, you've forgotten your wallet!*

*Flushed with embarrassment, you assure them that you (your assistant) will put a cashier's check in the mail first thing in the morning, but you simply must dash off to a pressing engagement at the Playboy mansion with a pair of 16-year-old, aspiring Victoria's Secret models.*

*As you glide out the door, your buddies will sputter in amazement, flabbergasted to have had the opportunity to luxuriate in the presence of such disarming spontaneity. Oh, to be so preoccupied up there in the dizzying ethers of the creative sphere that you could leave home without your wallet!*

*But, most important, you feel really good about yourself, for having so selflessly shared of your plentiful good fortune with a bunch of congenitally ordinary simpletons, who almost certainly lack even a hint of the panoramic awareness required to appreciate such an elegant gesture. Yet, even in their pedestrian stupidity, you observe with the hint of a smile, they will surely discuss you back at the office for days to come.*

*But, what was it you (your assistant) were going to put in the mail?*

## ABOUT *the* AUTHOR

William D. Wolff was a professional jazz/blues guitarist and composer prior to becoming a writer.

Mr. Wolff is the author of 2 award-winning screenplays, Soft Money and That's Afterlife!. He is currently working on a new screenplay, a book of short stories and a top-secret follow-up to Screenwriting four Geniuses.

Mr. Wolff is married to a writer and has two daughters, one a senior at American University in Washington, DC, and the other working towards her MFA at San Francisco State. Mr. Wolff lives in Los Angeles.